Personal Finance and Money Management

TOMMASO G. BERTONI

TABLE OF CONTENTS

«Money is vulgar, but wonderful. All I want in life is to make a lot of money and spend it».

(Freddie Mercury)

INTRODUCTION

by the Author

Welcome to the ebook "Personal Finance and Money Management." This book has been created to guide you through the complex world of personal finance, helping you develop the skills necessary to manage money effectively, plan for the future, and achieve lasting financial stability.

Personal finances are a crucial aspect of our daily lives because they not only impact our ability to cover daily expenses but also influence our future prospects and the quality of our lives. Learning to manage money is a fundamental yet often overlooked skill that can make a significant difference in our overall well-being.

In this ebook, we will explore various aspects of personal finance, from understanding money to the importance of financial awareness, from creating a budget to saving, from investments to debt management. Each chapter will take you through a different area of personal finance, providing clear information, practical tips, and tools that you can use in your daily life.

Remember that personal finances are a unique and individual journey. Your financial needs and goals may differ from those of others, and that's perfectly normal. The goal is to provide you with the knowledge and resources needed to make conscious financial decisions that align with your specific needs.

Financial management requires time, commitment, and patience, but the results can be rewarding. I hope this ebook helps you build a solid financial foundation, reduce money-related stress, and achieve greater financial stability. Let's begin the journey toward a better understanding of personal finances and more effective money management.

CHAPTER 1: UNDERSTANDING MONEY

Money is one of the most powerful and pervasive forces in our lives. It plays an essential role in every aspect of our existence, from meeting basic needs to achieving our loftiest dreams. Gaining a profound understanding of money is the first step toward wise financial management and a stable financial life. In this chapter, we will explore the meaning and value of money, the importance of being aware of our financial relationships, the various forms of money, and the crucial role that time plays in money management.

1.1 Definition of Money and Value

Money is a representation of value. It is a medium of exchange that allows us to obtain goods and services in exchange for an equivalent value. While we might envision money as coins and banknotes, it is important to understand that money goes beyond its physical form as it can exist digitally, in bank accounts, investments, or even in the form of property.

The value of money is a key concept to grasp. The value of money can vary over time and space. For example, the amount of goods and services you can acquire with a specific amount of money will change over time due to inflation. Additionally, the value of money may differ in some countries due to exchange rates.

1.2 The Importance of Financial Awareness

Financial awareness is an understanding of how money works and how it can be managed effectively. Being aware of our financial affairs is essential for making wise financial decisions. This includes the ability to create a budget, save, invest, and manage debt intelligently.

Being aware of our financial relationships allows us to avoid financial pitfalls and problems such as excessive debt, poor credit, and financial failure. Moreover, it enables us to recognize financial opportunities and plan for the future.

1.3 The Different Forms of Money

As mentioned earlier, money is not just cash. There are many different forms of money, including:

Cash: traditional coins and banknotes.

Bank deposits: money held in bank accounts, easily accessible through withdrawals or digital payments.

Investments: money invested in stocks, bonds, real estate, mutual funds, and other forms of investment.

Property: the value of real estate or personal assets we own.

Credit: access to money borrowed from financial institutions or creditors.

Each form of money has its unique characteristics and purpose. Understanding how these forms interact is fundamental to comprehensive and thoughtful financial management.

1.4 Time as a Key Factor

An often overlooked aspect of money management is time. It is a crucial factor when it comes to how money grows or diminishes in value. Two important principles related to time are compound interest and inflation.

Compound Interest: This principle tells us that invested money grows faster over time as earned interest is reinvested.

Inflation: Inflation reduces the purchasing power of money over time. This means that a sum of money today will have less purchasing power in ten or twenty years.

Understanding the role of time in money management allows us to make more foresighted financial decisions. Investing money wisely and safeguarding against inflation become crucial aspects of financial planning.

Money is a powerful force that influences every aspect of our lives. Understanding money, its value, and the importance of financial awareness is fundamental to wise financial management. In the next chapter, we will explore how to create an effective budget and plan personal finances for a stable and secure future.

CHAPTER 2: BUDGETING AND FINANCIAL PLANNING

Financial planning is at the core of the concept of responsible personal finance. Without a solid financial plan, it's easy to find oneself living beyond one's means and accumulating debt. In this chapter, we will examine the importance of creating a budget and how to plan effectively for the future.

The Importance of Budgeting

A budget is an essential financial tool that helps track income and expenses. It is a detailed list of planned expenses and anticipated income, enabling an understanding of where money goes and how to optimize it. Here are some key reasons why a budget is so crucial:

Financial Control: A budget gives you control over your financial situation. You can see exactly how much you spend and where. This is crucial to avoid impulsive spending and strategically plan expenses.

Planning: Creating a budget allows you to plan for the future. You can set clear financial goals and work towards them, whether it's saving for a home, children's education, or retirement. A budget helps you achieve these objectives.

Debt Reduction: A budget can be a powerful tool for debt reduction. It allows you to allocate additional funds for debt repayment, helping free yourself from financial worries.

Savings: Through a budget, you can plan your savings consistently. Setting aside a portion of your income is crucial for dealing with emergencies and building a savings fund.

Stress Reduction: Knowing how to manage money allows you to reduce financial stress, eliminating concerns about covering unforeseen expenses or increasing debts.

Creating an Effective Budget

Creating an effective budget requires some time and effort, but the benefits are numerous. Here's how to get started:

Gather Information: Start by collecting all necessary financial information, including income (salary, dividends, other sources) and expenses (rent or mortgage, bills, food expenses, debts).

List Expenses: Create a detailed list of your monthly expenses, categorizing them (e.g., housing, transportation, food, entertainment).

Calculate Monthly Income and Expenses: Sum up all your monthly income and expenses. Ensure that income exceeds expenses.

Set Financial Goals: Define short and long-term financial goals. These may include saving for a vacation, debt elimination, retirement savings, etc.

Allocate a Budget to Expense Categories: Once you know how much you earn and what your monthly expenses are, assign a budget to each category. Make sure to save or invest a portion of your income.

Monitor and Update the Budget: Regularly monitor how well you are adhering to the budget and make adjustments as necessary. You can use budgeting software or apps to streamline the process.

Plan for Emergencies: Ensure you have a category for unexpected expenses, so you don't have to dip into your main budget.

A well-planned budget is a powerful tool for achieving your financial well-being. It helps you stay in control, plan for the future, and reduce financial stress.

In this chapter, we have examined the importance of budgeting and how to create an effective one. In the upcoming chapters, we will explore further aspects of personal finance to help you achieve financial stability.

CHAPTER 3: SAVING AND INVESTMENTS

Saving and investments are two fundamental pillars for long-term financial success. In this chapter, we will explore the importance of saving, different ways to save money, and how to begin investing intelligently to grow your wealth.

The Importance of Saving

Saving is the foundation of a strong financial situation. Here's why it's so crucial:

Emergencies: Saved money can cover unexpected expenses like car repairs, unforeseen medical bills, or job loss, protecting you from burdensome debts in challenging situations.

Future Planning: Saving is essential for achieving long-term goals such as buying a home, providing for children's education, or retirement.

Reduced Stress: Having savings allows you to reduce stress related to financial matters. You won't constantly worry about covering essential expenses.

Financial Independence: Saved money gives you the freedom to make financial choices, such as changing jobs, starting a business, or taking a sabbatical.

How to Save Money

Saving begins with adopting responsible financial habits. Here are some strategies to save money:

Create a Budget: Use a budget to track income and expenses. This helps identify areas where expenses can be cut.

Automate Savings: Set up an automatic transfer to a savings account every time you receive payment. This compels you to save before spending.

Cut Unnecessary Expenses: Review monthly expenses and identify those that can be reduced or eliminated. This might include restaurant expenses, unnecessary subscriptions, or other luxuries.

Negotiate Rates: Don't hesitate to negotiate with service providers, such as the phone company or insurance, to get better rates.

Automatic Savings on Windfalls: When you receive a raise or an unexpected sum of money, don't immediately increase expenses. Allocate a portion of these earnings to savings or investments.

Investments as a Tool for Financial Growth

While saving is fundamental, investments are a means to grow your wealth. Investing your money allows you to earn interest or returns and achieve long-term financial gains. Here are some common investment options:

Stocks: Investing in stocks means buying a share of a company. Stocks can appreciate in value and distribute dividends.

Bonds: Bonds are debt securities issued by governments or companies. They provide regular interest payments and return of capital.

Mutual Funds: These funds pool money from various investors to buy a variety of stocks and bonds. They are managed by financial professionals.

Real Estate: Investing in real estate can involve purchasing properties or participating in real estate funds.

Retirement Savings: Contributing to retirement savings plans can provide tax benefits and financial growth opportunities.

Getting Started with Investing

To begin investing, it's essential to educate yourself about different available options and your risk tolerance. Here are some guidelines to start:

Conduct Research: Learn more about various investment options and consider diversification, spreading money across different assets.

Consult a Professional: Seek the help of a financial advisor or investment consultant for expert guidance.

Start Early: Compound interest is a powerful ally for long-term investors. Starting early increases growth potential.

Monitor and Adjust: Once you've started investing, regularly monitor your investments and make adjustments based on changes in your financial needs and investment goals.

Saving and investments are key elements for financial stability and achieving long-term financial goals. In this chapter, we have examined the importance of saving, strategies for saving money, and various investment options available. In the upcoming sections, we will explore further aspects of personal finance to help you build a solid financial foundation and plan for the future.

CHAPTER 4: DEBT MANAGEMENT

Debt management is a critical aspect of your personal finances. In this chapter, we will explore its importance and examine different types of debt along with strategies to effectively reduce and manage it.

The Importance of Debt Management

Debt can become a financial burden if not handled correctly. Here's why debt management is essential:

Avoid High Interest: Debts with high-interest rates, such as credit card debts, can accumulate significant interest over time. Debt management helps minimize these costs.

Maintain Healthy Credit: A good credit score is crucial for obtaining future loans and financing on favorable terms. Debt management helps preserve your credit score.

Reduce Financial Stress: Excessive debt can cause stress and financial worries. Effective debt management lessens the weight of these concerns.

Types of Debt

There are various types of debt, each with its own characteristics and financial implications. Here are some common types:

Credit Cards: This is a revolving type of debt with high-interest rates. Paying the full monthly balance is the best way to avoid high interest.

Student Loans: Loans for education can be helpful, but it's important to plan repayment to avoid excessive financial burden.

Mortgages: A mortgage is a long-term loan used to purchase a home. Managing the mortgage is essential to prevent foreclosure.

Personal Loans: These loans can be used for various purposes but often come with higher interest rates compared to other types of debt.

Auto Loans: Financing a car is a common type of debt. Managing auto debt involves timely and complete payments.

Strategies to Reduce and Manage Debt

Here are some strategies to effectively reduce and manage debt:

Create a Repayment Plan: Start with a repayment plan that includes regular debt payments. This plan should be based on your financial budget.

Prioritize: If you have multiple debts, consider focusing on paying off those with the highest interest rates to save money on interest.

Negotiate Interest Rates: In some cases, you may be able to negotiate lower interest rates with your creditors.

Debt Consolidation: Debt consolidation involves combining various debts into one with a lower interest rate.

Use Windfalls for Debt Payment: Use extra money or bonuses to pay off debt instead of spending on non-essential expenses.
Build an Emergency Fund: Having an emergency fund helps avoid

accumulating additional debt in case of unexpected expenses.

Long-Term Planning

Debt management is not just about reducing current debts but also preventing future debt issues. It's essential to develop a solid financial foundation and practice responsible financial management.

In conclusion, debt management is crucial for financial stability. Reducing debt and adopting healthy financial habits put you on the path to a strong financial situation and the achievement of your long-term financial goals. In the next chapter, we will explore further aspects of personal finance to help you build a solid financial foundation and ensure a healthy financial future.

CHAPTER 5: CREDITS AND CREDIT

Credit is a significant aspect of your personal finances and can influence your ability to obtain loans, mortgages, and credit cards on favorable terms. In this chapter, we will explore the meaning of credit, how it works, its impact on your financial situation, and how to manage it responsibly.

Understanding Credit

Credit is essentially the trust that a person or financial institution extends to lend you money or provide goods and services now in exchange for future payment. It operates as follows:

Credit Application: When applying for a loan or credit card, the creditor assesses your financial profile to determine your eligibility for credit.

Credit Approval: If you meet the creditor's requirements, credit is approved, granting you access to funds or the offered goods or services.

Credit Utilization: After obtaining credit, you can use it to make purchases or meet other financial needs.

Repayment: You must then repay the borrowed money or pay for the goods or services within the agreed-upon period, often with respective interest.

The Importance of Credit

Credit is important for various reasons:

Access to Financing: Good credit provides access to loans and financing for significant purchases such as homes, cars, and education.

Favorable Interest Rates: A good credit score allows you to obtain loans at lower interest rates, saving money on interest payments.

Credit Cards: Good credit qualifies you for credit cards with higher limits and better benefits.

Leasing: A good credit score can facilitate obtaining a lease for an apartment or house.

Credit Report

Your credit report is a record of your credit activities, containing information about credit cards, loans, and other forms of credit, as well as your payments and financial behavior.

Credit Score

The credit score is a number representing your financial reliability. Common credit scores include the FICO score and VantageScore. These scores consider various factors, including:

Payment History: Timely payments are crucial for maintaining a good credit score.

Existing Debt: Ongoing debt, especially near credit limits, can negatively impact the score.

Credit History: A long and positive credit history contributes to a higher score.

New Credit Lines: Opening new credit lines can have a temporary impact on the credit score.

Responsible Credit Management

Responsible credit management is essential to preserve and improve your credit score. Here are some guidelines:

Timely Payments: Ensure payments for loans, credit cards, and other credit lines are made on time.

Debt Control: Keep track of the amount of debt relative to credit limits and aim to keep it low.

Avoid Bad Credit: Steer clear of accumulating uncollectible debts, such as defaulted loans or bankruptcies.

Monitor Credit Report: Regularly check your credit report for any errors or suspicious activities.

Credit management requires discipline and financial responsibility. A good credit score is a valuable financial tool that can provide you with significant opportunities and advantages. In the next chapter, we will explore how to plan for financial futures and establish short and long-term financial goals.

CHAPTER 6: PLANNING FOR THE FUTURE

Planning for your financial future is a crucial part of personal finance management. Without a well-defined strategy for your money, you might find yourself living beyond your means, unable to save for important or unexpected goals. In this chapter, we will understand how to plan, set financial goals, and create a solid financial plan.

Setting Financial Goals

The first step in planning is establishing clear and realistic financial goals. These goals should cover various areas of your financial life, including:

Financial Emergencies: Save in an emergency fund to cover unexpected expenses such as emergency repairs or medical bills.

Retirement: Planning for retirement is essential to ensure a stable financial future.

Education: If you have children or plan to continue your education, you should plan for these expenses.

Homeownership: If you dream of owning a home, you need a financial plan to save for the purchase.

Investments: Consider how you want to invest your money to

make it grow over time.

Creating a Budget

A budget is an essential tool in financial planning. It allows you to track your income, expenses, and how you are saving for financial goals. To create an effective budget, follow these steps:

Calculate Income: Begin by listing all sources of income, including salaries, dividends, and other sources of money.

List Expenses: Record all your monthly expenses, including rent or mortgage, bills, food expenses, transportation, and other regular expenses.

Define Goals: Establish how much you want to save each month for each financial goal. Ensure these savings allocations are realistic and sustainable.

Monitor the Budget: Track expenses throughout the month and compare them with the planned budget. This will allow you to make any necessary corrections.

Saving and Investments

Saving is a key component in financial planning. Saving not only for emergencies but also for short and long-term goals helps build financial stability. Consider opening specific savings accounts for each goal, such as an emergency fund or retirement fund.

Investments are another important aspect. As your savings grow, consider investing in stocks, bonds, mutual funds, or other financial instruments. Investments can grow your wealth over time but also come with a certain level of risk.

Debt Reduction

Debt reduction is a critical aspect of financial planning. If you have significant debts, work on a plan to pay them off. Try to lower interest rates, establish a repayment plan, and aim to pay more than required each month.

Monitor and Adapt

Financial planning is an evolving process. Constantly monitor your budget, progress towards goals, and the performance of your investments. If necessary, make adjustments to your financial plan to reflect changes in your life or goals.

A solid financial plan is essential to ensure economic security and the achievement of your goals. Regardless of your current situation, start planning for the future today to build a strong financial foundation for yourself and your family.

In the next chapter, we will explore strategies to protect your assets and ensure long-term financial well-being.

CHAPTER 7: DEALING WITH FINANCIAL EMERGENCIES

Financial emergencies can strike anyone at any time. A sudden medical issue, job loss, or costly repairs can test your financial stability. In this chapter, we will explore how to face financial emergencies responsibly and strategically.

Preparation for Emergencies

The first line of defense against financial emergencies is foresight. Before facing any crisis, you should implement some preventive measures:

Emergency Fund: An emergency fund is a reserve of money you should have on hand to cover unexpected expenses. The primary purpose of this fund is to cover essential expenses such as rent or mortgage, bills, and food for a period of at least three to six months. Start building it gradually by setting aside a small amount of money each month.

Insurance: Secure adequate insurance to cover medical emergencies, accidents, or property losses. Good insurance coverage can save you a lot in case of an emergency.

Financial Plan: Having a well-structured financial plan with clear goals helps maintain a financial safety net.

Facing Emergencies

If you find yourself in a financial emergency, follow these steps:

Stay Calm: Fear and panic can lead to impulsive and harmful financial decisions. It is essential to remain calm and approach the situation rationally.

Evaluate the Situation: Analyze the financial situation and determine the severity of the emergency. Consider how much money will be needed to address it.

Use the Emergency Fund: If you have an emergency fund, it is time to use it. Use it judiciously and only for essential expenses.

Contact Creditors: If you are concerned about debts or impending payments, contact creditors. Many companies are willing to work with you to find temporary solutions during emergencies.

Explore Loan Options: If the emergency fund is insufficient, consider options like personal loans or credit cards. Be cautious not to accumulate too much debt and seek possibilities with the lowest interest rates.

Cut Expenses: Trim non-essential expenses during the emergency. Cut unnecessary costs and focus on essential spending.

Seek Assistance: If facing long-term financial hardship, seek assistance from local social services, charities, or financial counseling agencies.

Prevention for the Future

After dealing with a financial emergency, it is crucial to learn from the situation and take steps to prevent a future one:

Reflect on the Cause: Reflect on the cause of the emergency and how you can avoid it in the future. For example, if the emergency was due to job loss, consider expanding your skills or diversifying your sources of income.

Save More: After facing an emergency, you might be more motivated to save more for your emergency fund.

Adequate Insurance: Evaluate if your insurance coverages are adequate and, if necessary, make changes to ensure greater financial security.

Debt Control: Continue working on the debt repayment plan to reduce indebtedness.

Financial emergencies are inevitable in life, but with proper planning and a responsible response, they can be effectively addressed. Prepare with an emergency fund, stay calm during crises, and learn from your experience to avoid future financial difficulties.

In the next chapter, we will explore how to protect your assets and ensure long-term financial well-being.

CHAPTER 8: IMPROVING YOUR FINANCIAL HABITS

Improving your financial habits is a fundamental step to ensure long-term financial well-being. Your daily choices and financial decisions can have a significant impact on your economic situation. In this chapter, we will discover how to identify and change negative financial habits and develop new ones that will help you achieve your financial goals.

Identifying Wrong Financial Habits

The first step in improving your financial habits is to identify the negative ones. These habits can vary from person to person, but some of the most common ones include:

Impulsive Spending: Unplanned and impulsive purchases that can harm your budget.

Lack of Budgeting: Not having a budget or disregarding established spending limits.

High-Interest Payments: Excessive use of credit cards with high-interest rates.

Lack of Savings: Not setting aside a portion of your income in a savings or investment account.

Lack of Long-Term Planning: Failure to engage in long-term financial planning.

Poor Debt Control: Continuing to accumulate debt without a repayment plan.

Ignoring Bills: Ignoring bill due dates or debt payments.

Creating New Financial Habits

Once you've identified negative financial habits, it's time to develop new ones that will help improve your financial situation. Here are some strategies to do so:

Create a Budget: Establish a detailed monthly budget that takes into account all your income and expenses. Follow the budget and regularly review it to ensure compliance.

Save Automatically: Set up an automatic transfer to put aside a portion of your income into a savings or investment account.

Reduce Impulsive Expenses: Before making an impulsive purchase, take time to reflect on whether it is truly necessary and fits within the budget.

Debt Repayment: If you have debts, create a repayment plan and focus on reducing the debt as quickly as possible.

Long-Term Planning: Set long-term financial goals and develop a plan to achieve them.

Monitor Your Expenses: Keep track of your daily expenses to have a clear view of where your money is going.

Maintain Discipline

Improving financial habits requires discipline and constant commitment. Here are some tips to maintain discipline:

Be Consistent: Practice the new habits consistently, even when it may seem challenging or inconvenient.

Rewards: Acknowledge your financial successes and reward yourself with small incentives for a job well done.

Accountability: Share your financial goals with a friend or family member who can hold you accountable.

Education: Continue to educate yourself on personal finances and seek new ways to enhance your habits.

Improving your financial habits is crucial to achieving your financial goals and ensuring your long-term well-being. Identify and address negative financial habits, replace them with positive and responsible habits, and maintain discipline and consistency over time. You will see significant improvements in your financial situation.

CHAPTER 9: CONCLUSIONS

As you conclude this journey through the realm of personal finance and money management, you've gained fundamental knowledge and skills to enhance your financial situation and build a financially secure future. Throughout this path, we delved into the following themes:

Understanding Money: We explored the nature of money, its significance, and how it influences our lives. Understanding money is the first step toward controlling your finances.

Budgeting and Financial Planning: You learned to create a budget, follow a financial plan, and manage your financial resources effectively.

Saving and Investments: You discovered the importance of saving and investing for wealth creation and long-term financial security.

Debt Management: We discussed strategies to address and responsibly reduce debt.

Credits and Credit: You learned how to manage your credit wisely to build a solid financial foundation.

Planning for the Future: We explored retirement planning, long-term investments, and strategies to ensure a financially secure future.

Facing Financial Emergencies: You discovered how to prepare for financial emergencies and effectively handle them when they arise.

Improving Your Financial Habits: Finally, we discussed how to identify and change negative financial habits to improve your financial situation.

Now, it's essential to put into practice what you've learned. Success in personal finances requires dedication, consistency, and responsibility. Here are some final considerations for your journey toward financial well-being:

Planning and Consistency: Continue to plan and follow your financial plan consistently. Remember that small daily actions have a long-term impact.

Financial Education: Keep your thirst for financial knowledge alive. Ongoing information is crucial to staying abreast of an evolving financial world.

Saving and Investment: Save regularly and look for investment opportunities to grow your wealth.

Planning for the Future: Plan for the future, including your retirement. Start as early as possible to benefit from compound interest.

Facing Emergencies: Keep setting aside an emergency fund and face emergencies with calmness and discipline.

Financial Habits: Be aware of your financial habits and make necessary changes to improve them.

Sharing: Share your financial knowledge with others. Financial information is a valuable asset to spread.

Celebrate Success: Recognize and celebrate your financial successes, no matter how small.

Maintain Focus: Keep your long-term financial goal as a constant guide.

Remember, financial well-being is a tool for leading a fulfilling and meaningful life. You can adapt this knowledge and skills to your personal needs and goals. Maintain your determination and commitment to pursue a stable financial future.

Wishing you a financially secure and fulfilling future. Living without financial worries is a step toward a life full of opportunities and accomplishments.

TITLES BY THE SAME AUTHOR

Mind Manipulation and Persuasion Techniques: A Quick and Agile Guide to All the Secrets of Mind Manipulation and the Best Persuasion Techniques: If you want to improve your personal and professional life, train with the practical exercises and apply the advice in this manual. You will be able to maximize your communication skills, effectively managing friendships and professional relationships. Available exclusively on Amazon in Italian and soon in English.

Live Fearlessly: A Guide to Managing Anxiety and Stress: In the hustle and bustle of modern life, stress and anxiety can become constant companions, but they don't have to be the protagonists of your story. *Live Fearlessly: Managing Stress and Anxiety* is the comprehensive guide that will take you on a journey of self-discovery, balance, and emotional well-being. This book provides a clear and practical overview of key strategies to address and overcome stress and anxiety. Available exclusively on Amazon in Italian and English.

Awaken Your Potential: A Guide to Personal Development: Are you ready to embark on a journey of personal transformation? Do you want to uncover your limitless potential and live a life without boundaries? This book is your comprehensive guide to self-discovery and personal development. Don't wait! It's time to awaken your potential and live the life you deserve. Available exclusively on Amazon in Italian and English.

How to Create a New Online Job After 40: In "How to Create a New Online Job After 40," we delve into the exciting and inspirational journey of reinventing oneself professionally in a continually evolving digital era. From the world of online work to investment strategies, this book offers a comprehensive guide for anyone looking to transform their career and embrace new opportunities after the age of 40. With practical approaches, it will lead you through a path of personal discovery and professional growth. Get ready to embark on a new career adventure that aligns with your passions and skills, creating a rewarding and fulfilling professional future. Available exclusively on Amazon in Italian and English.